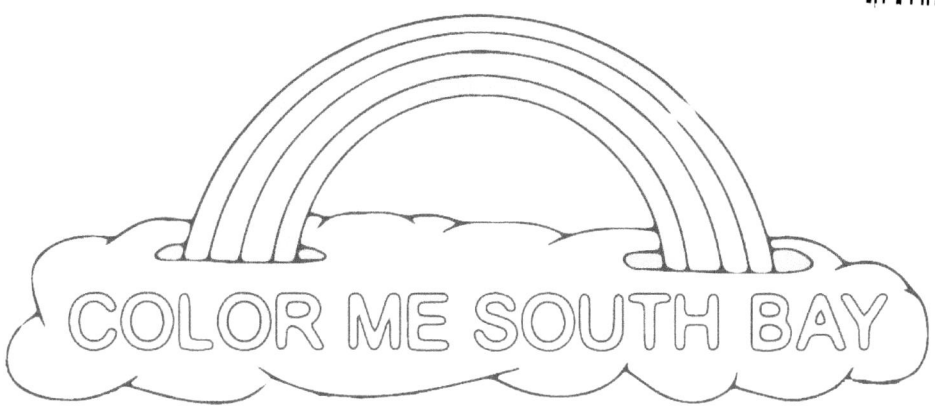

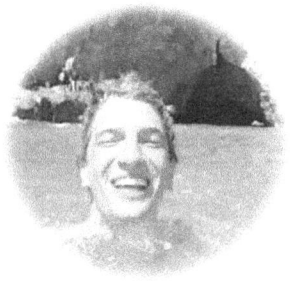

The South Bay, a region of Los Angeles' southwest peninsula, comprises the span from Palos Verdes to Manhattan Beach. It's a thriving home to surfing, volleyball, bike-riding and live music. Tightly packed beach cities, each with their own unique communities and culture, are hidden gems that I was fortunate enough to stumble upon after graduating college. With fun scenes and action doodles I created this coloring book for all ages to give everyone a chance to share this joy and appreciation for the South Bay and life in general.

Enjoy!

~Brian Michaud~

Bjmichaud90.wix.com/sticklamp

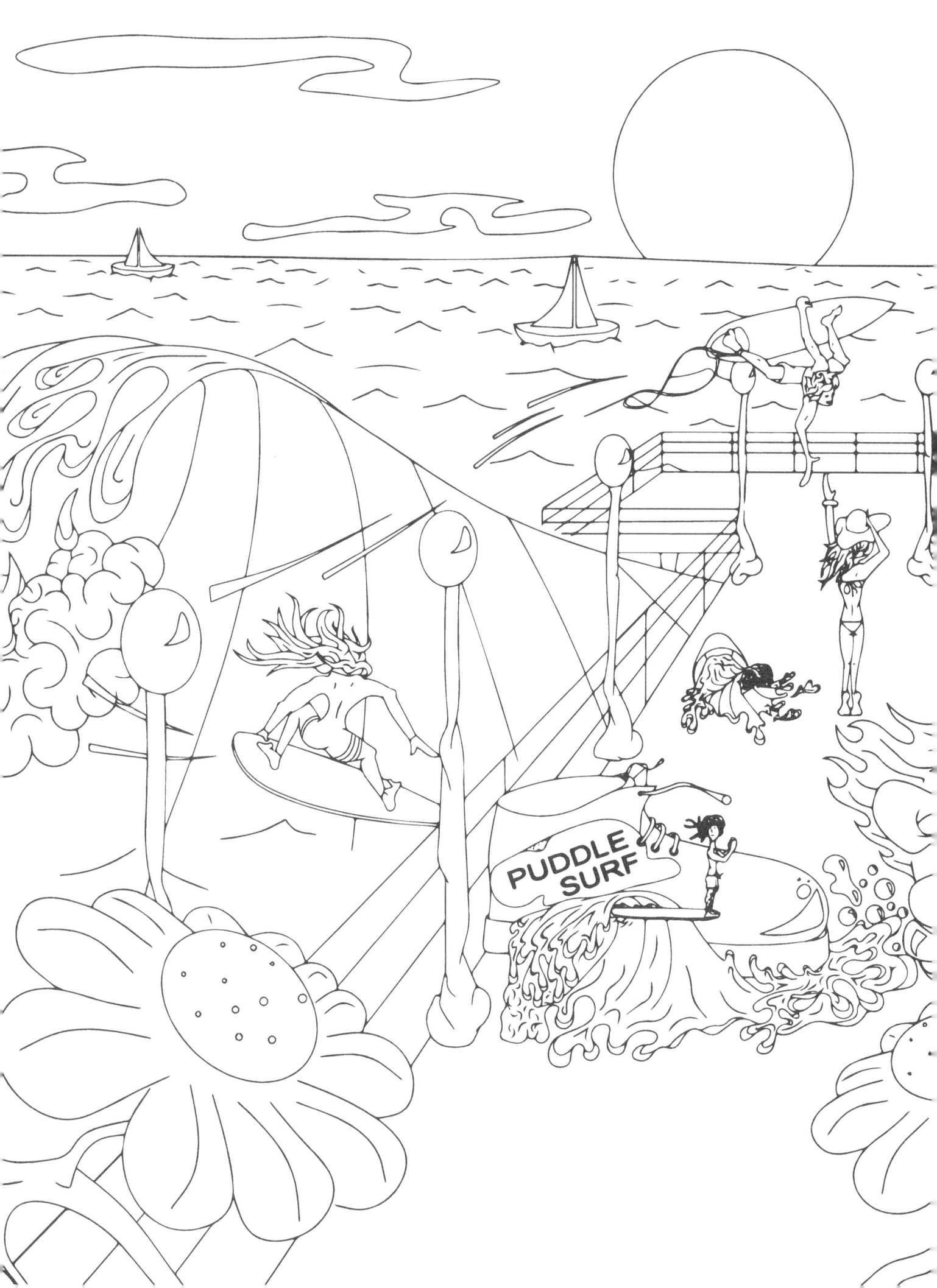

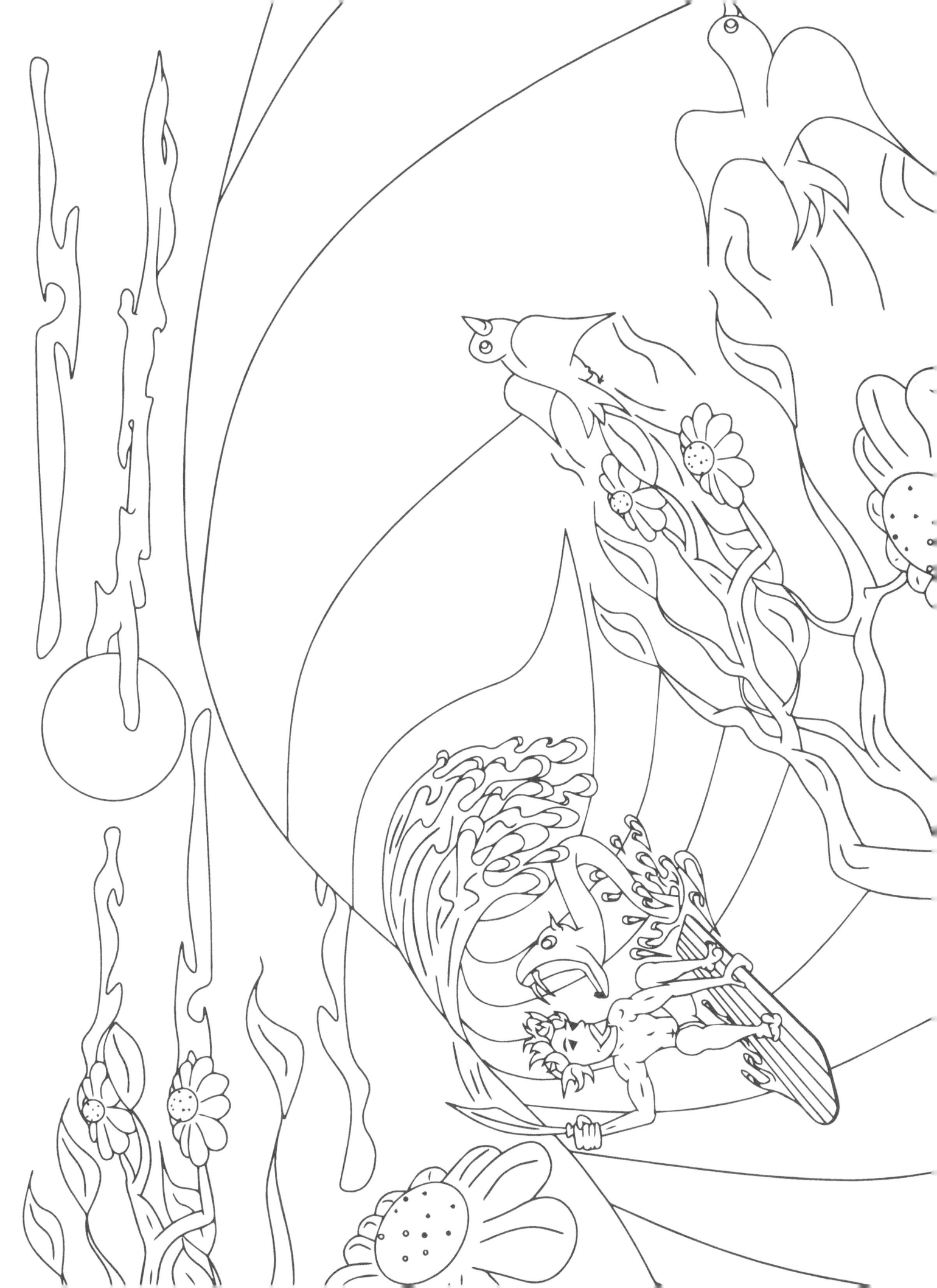

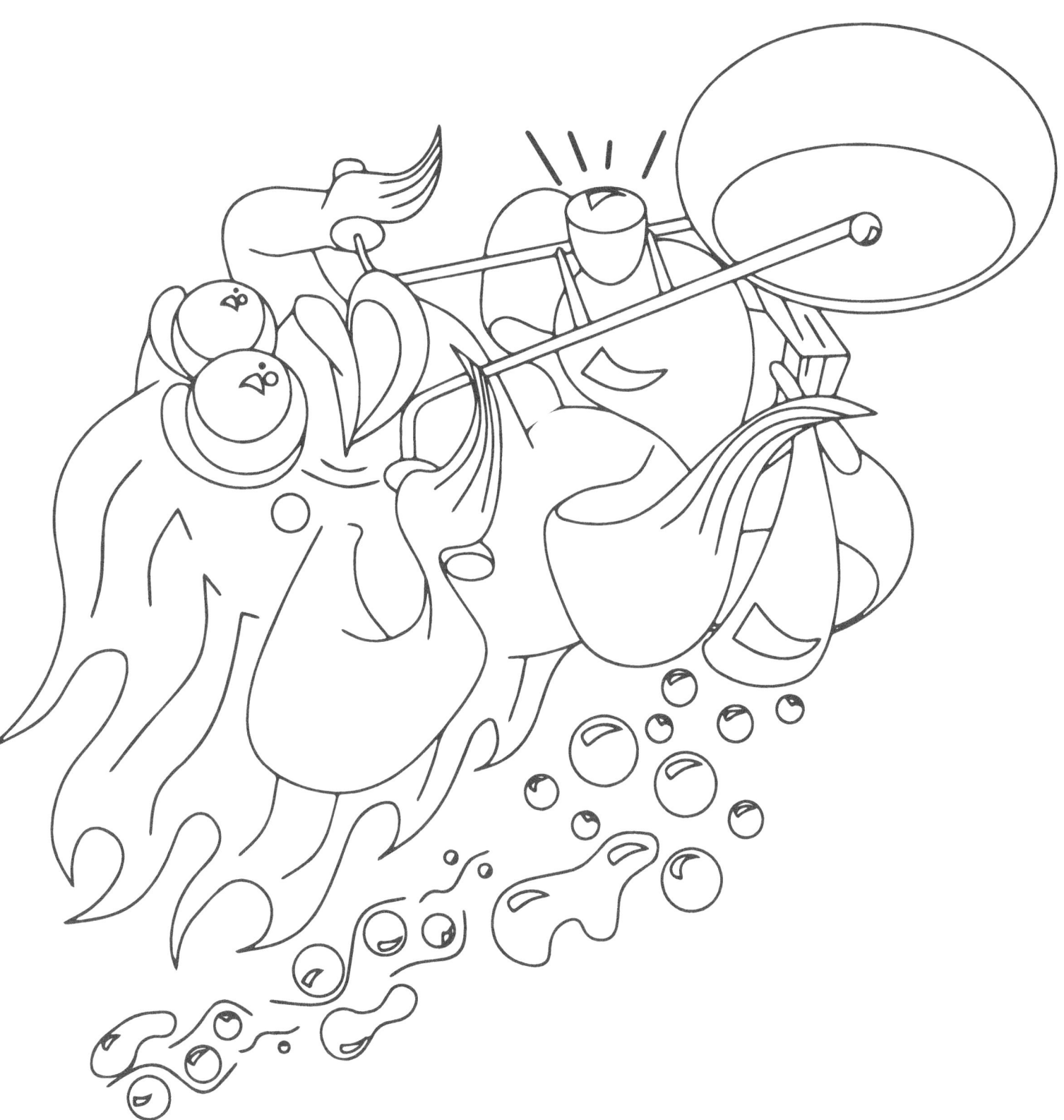

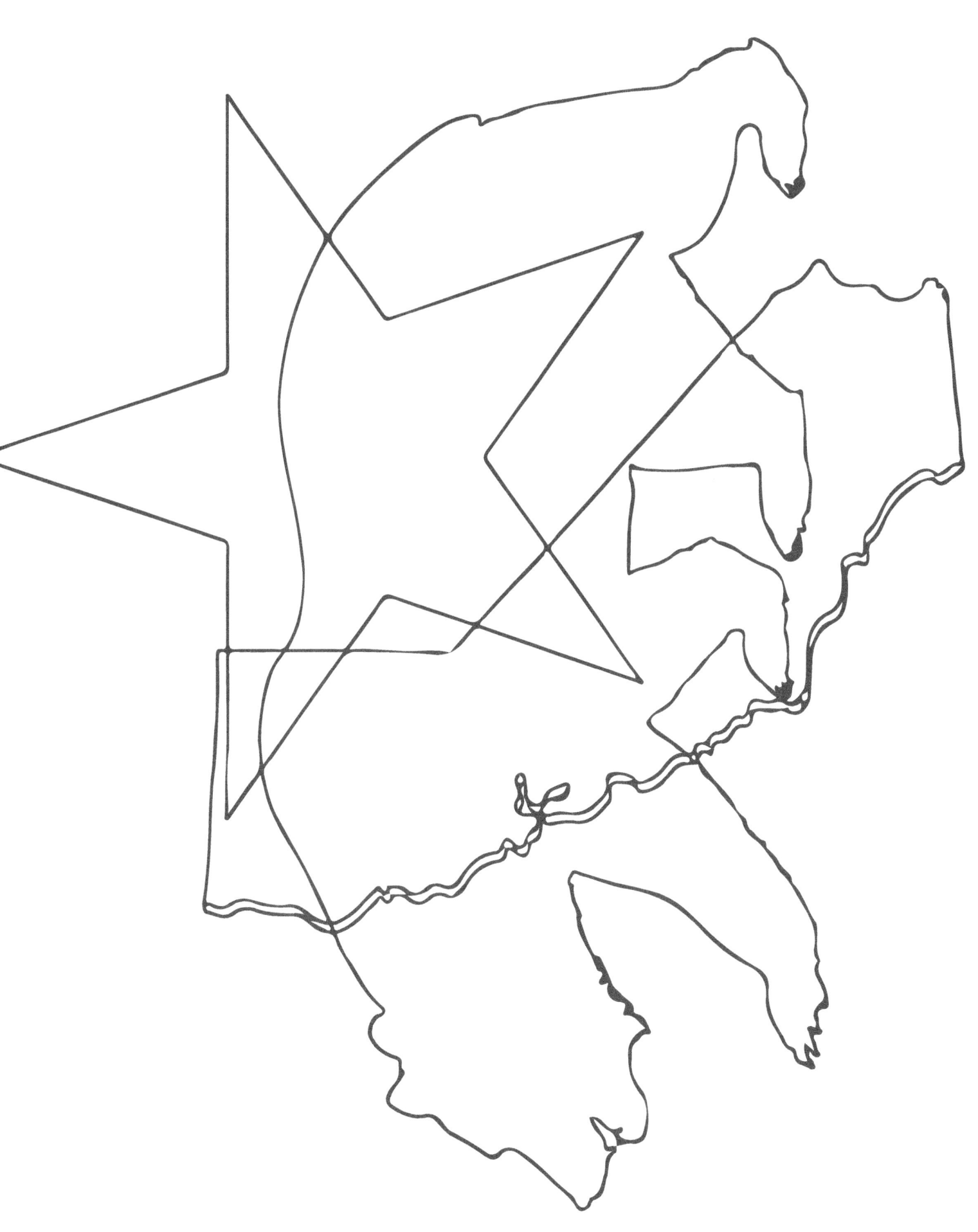

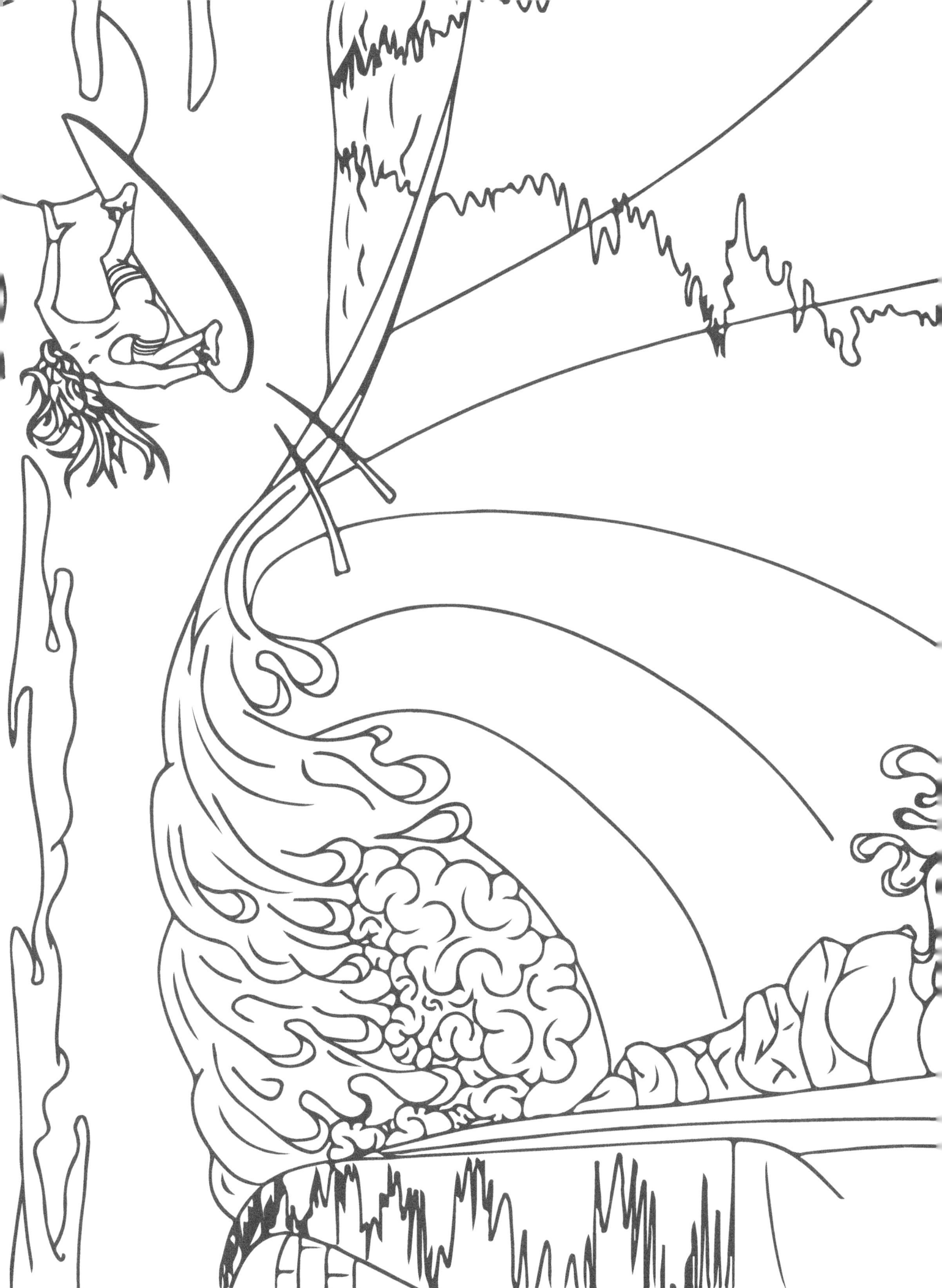

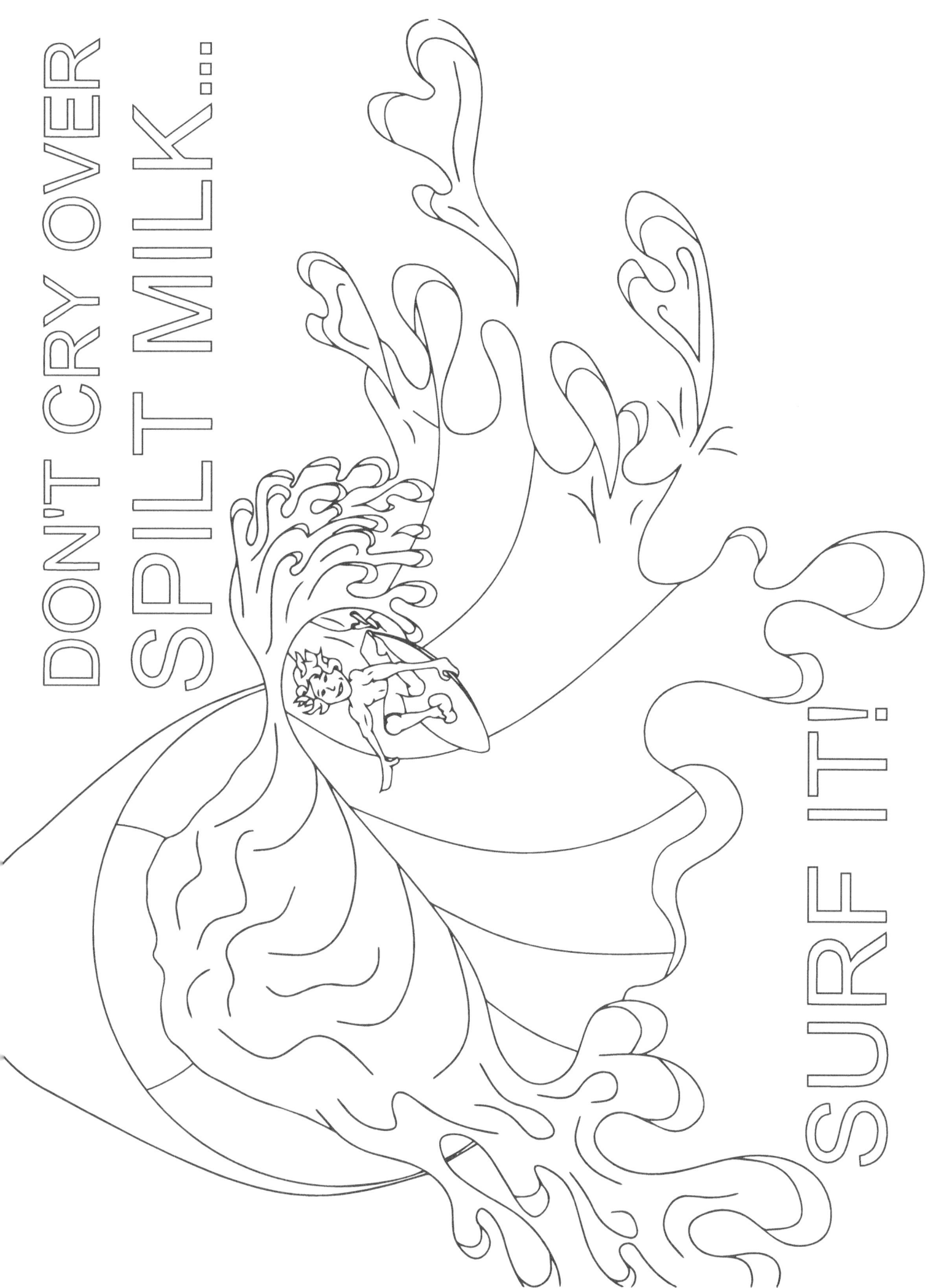

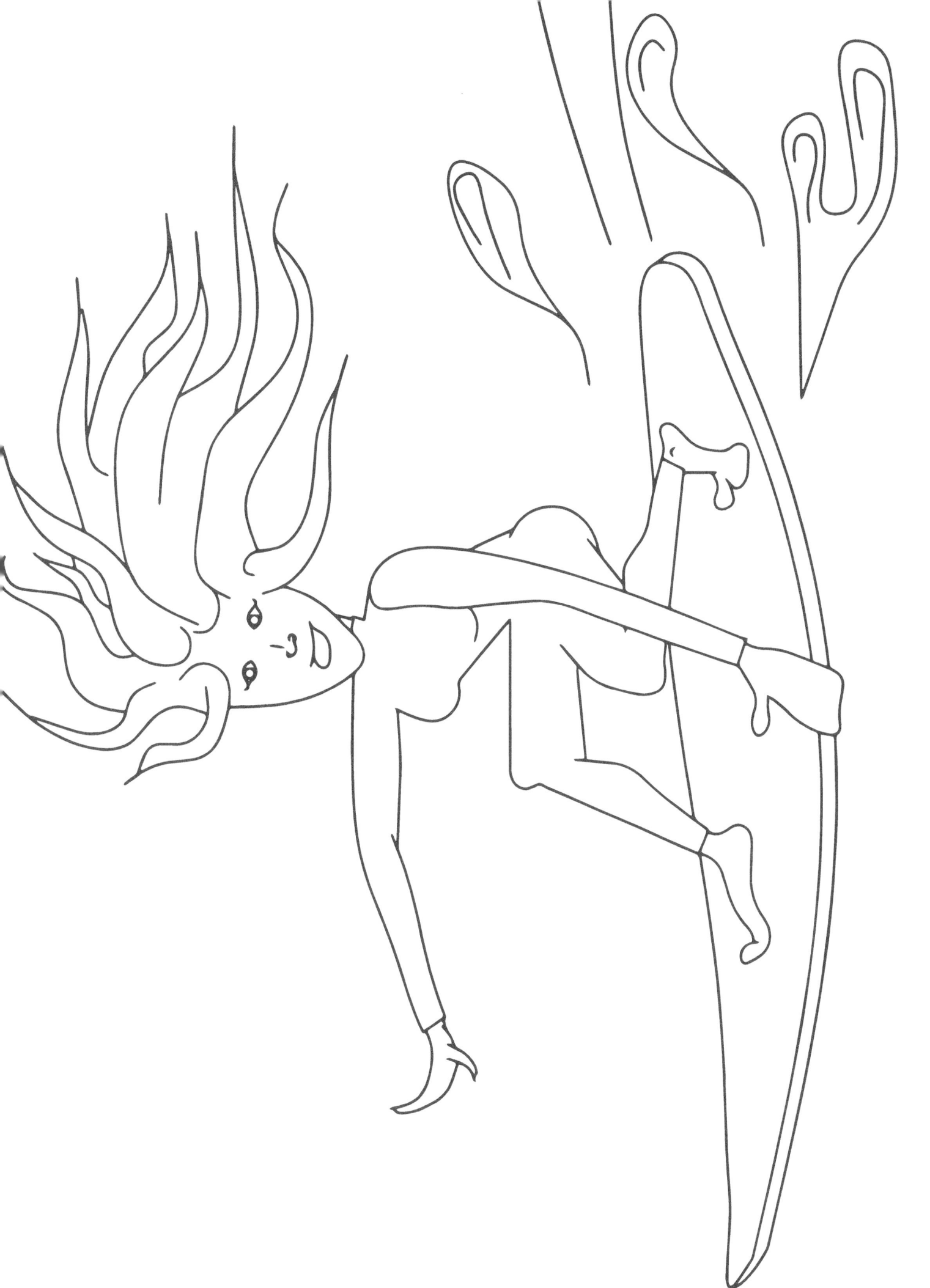

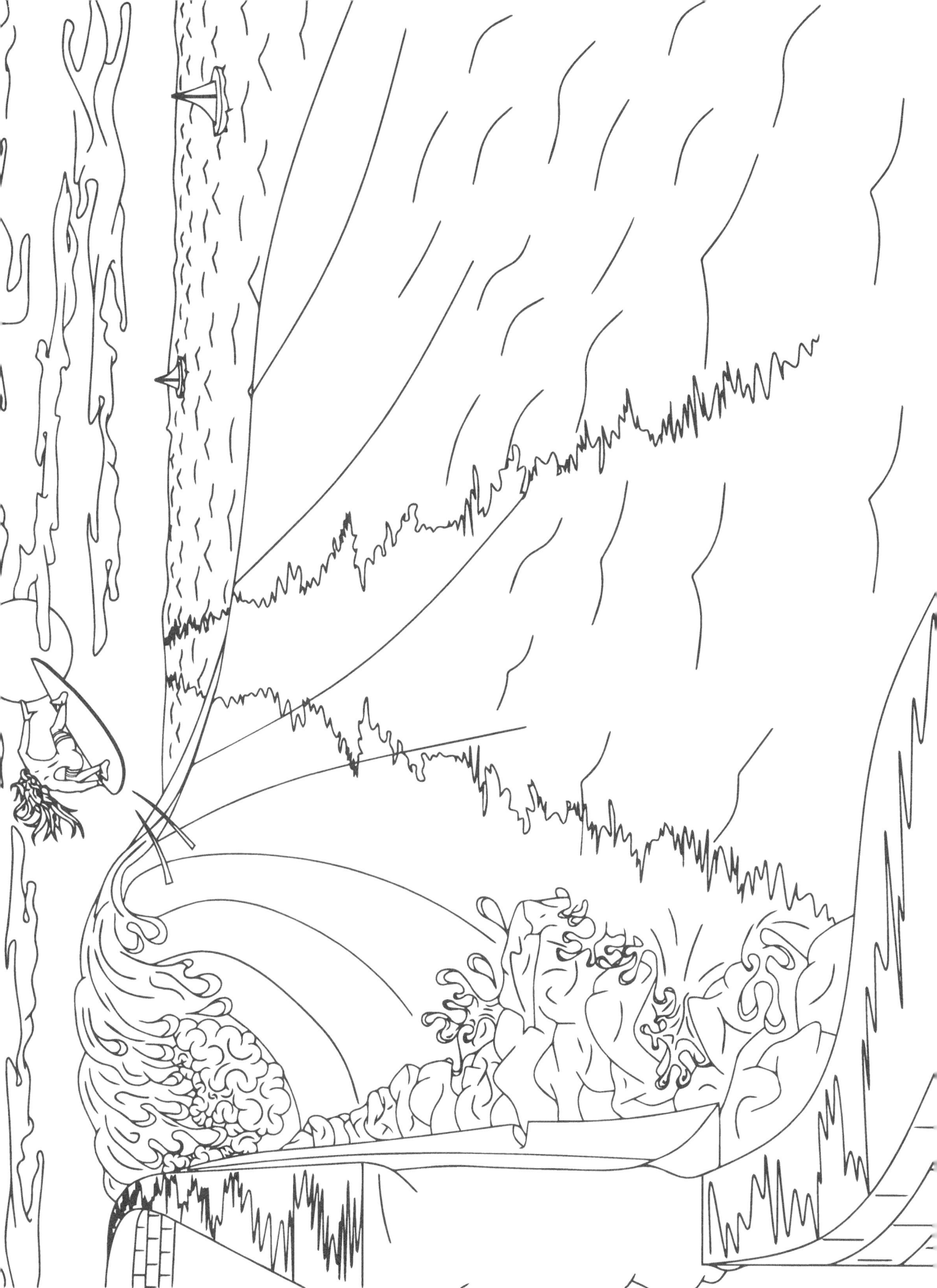

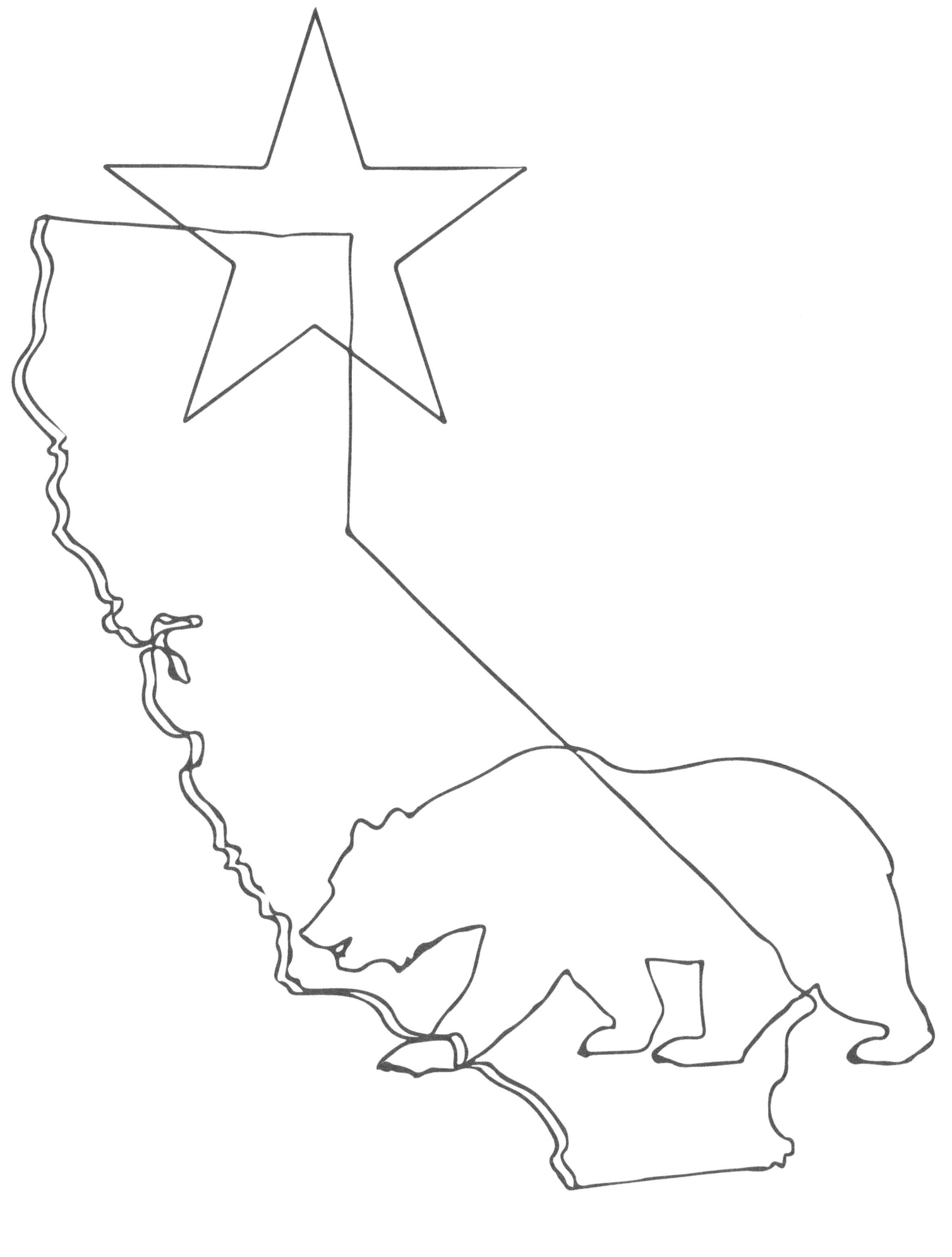

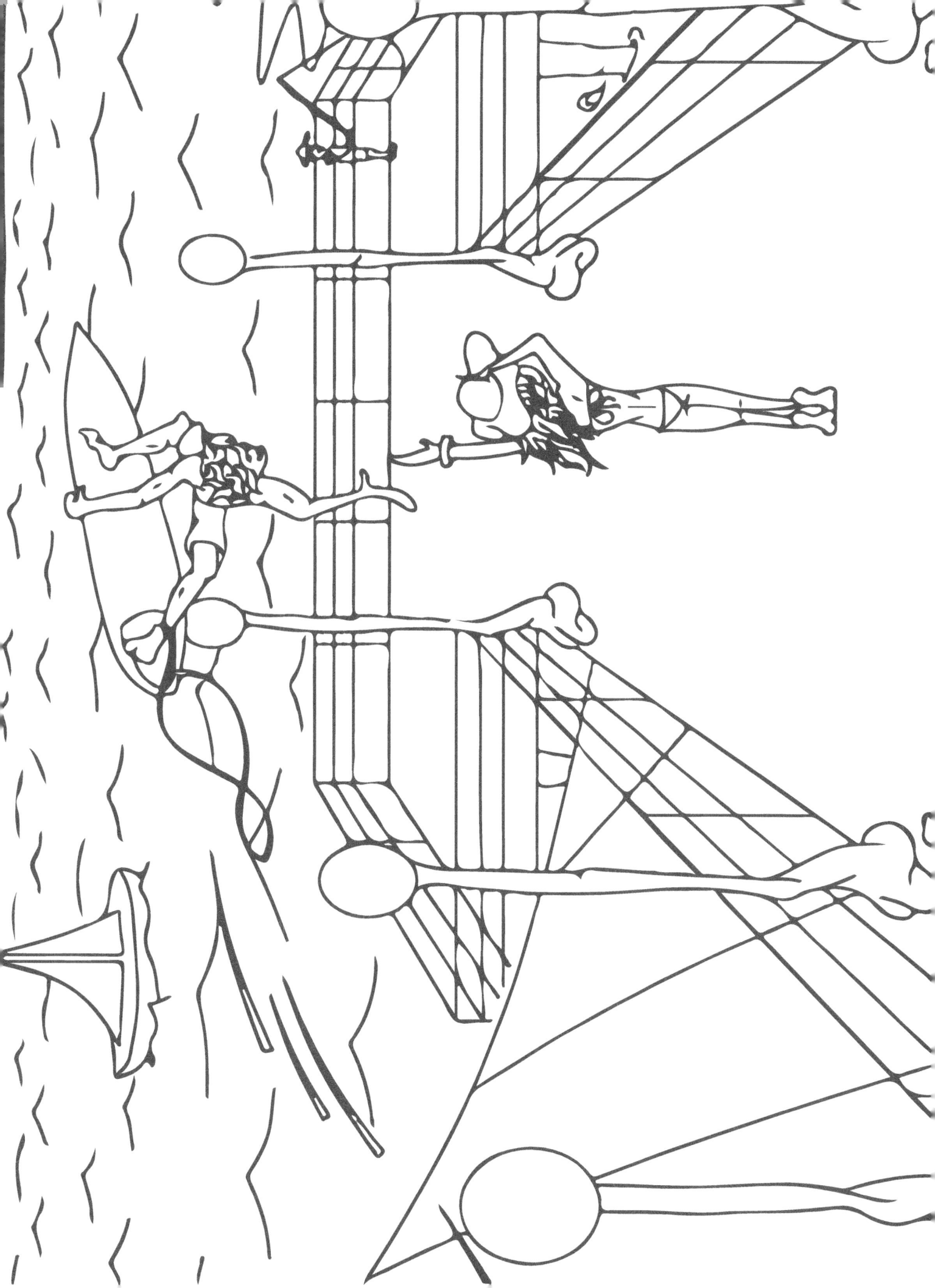

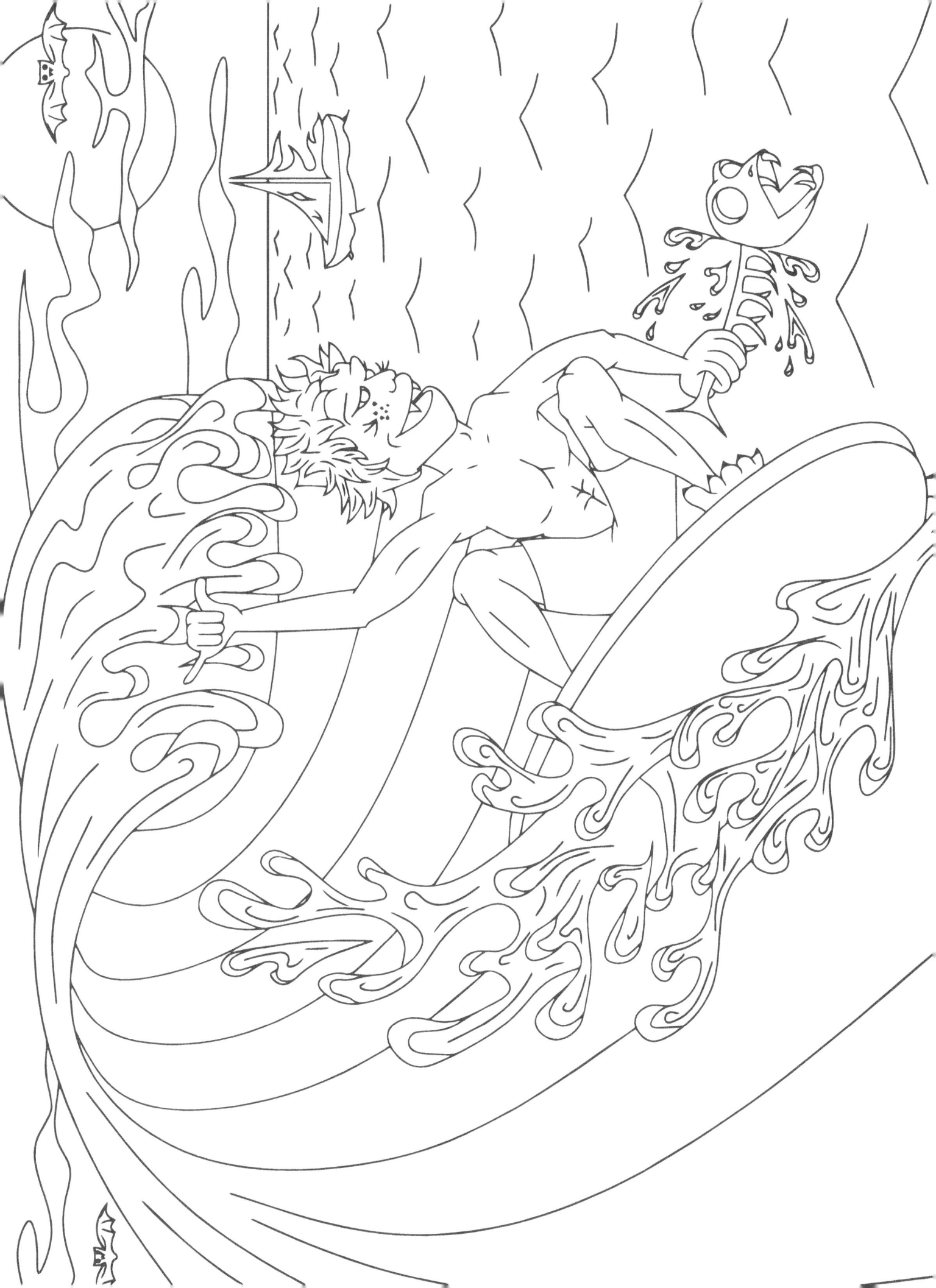

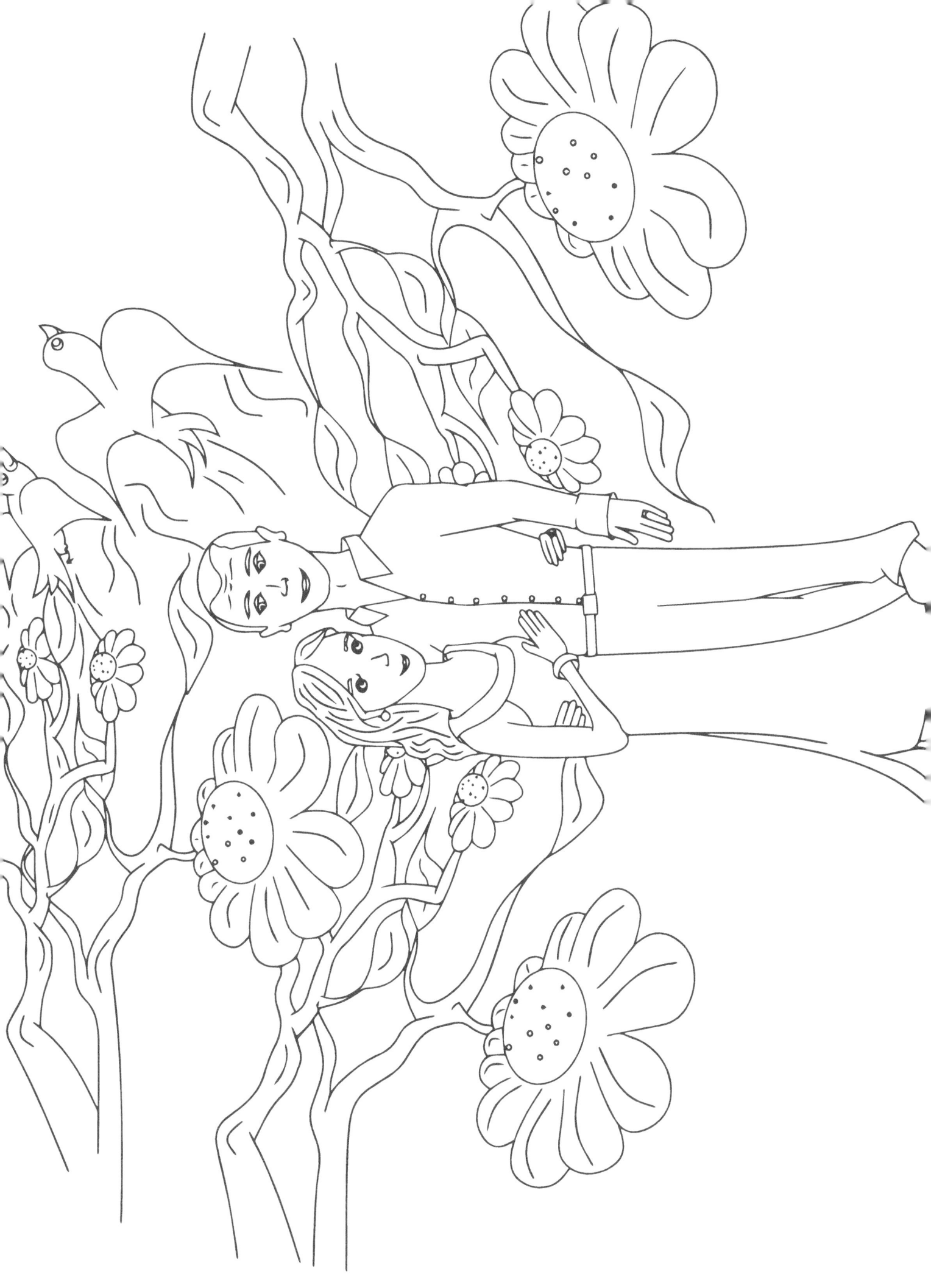

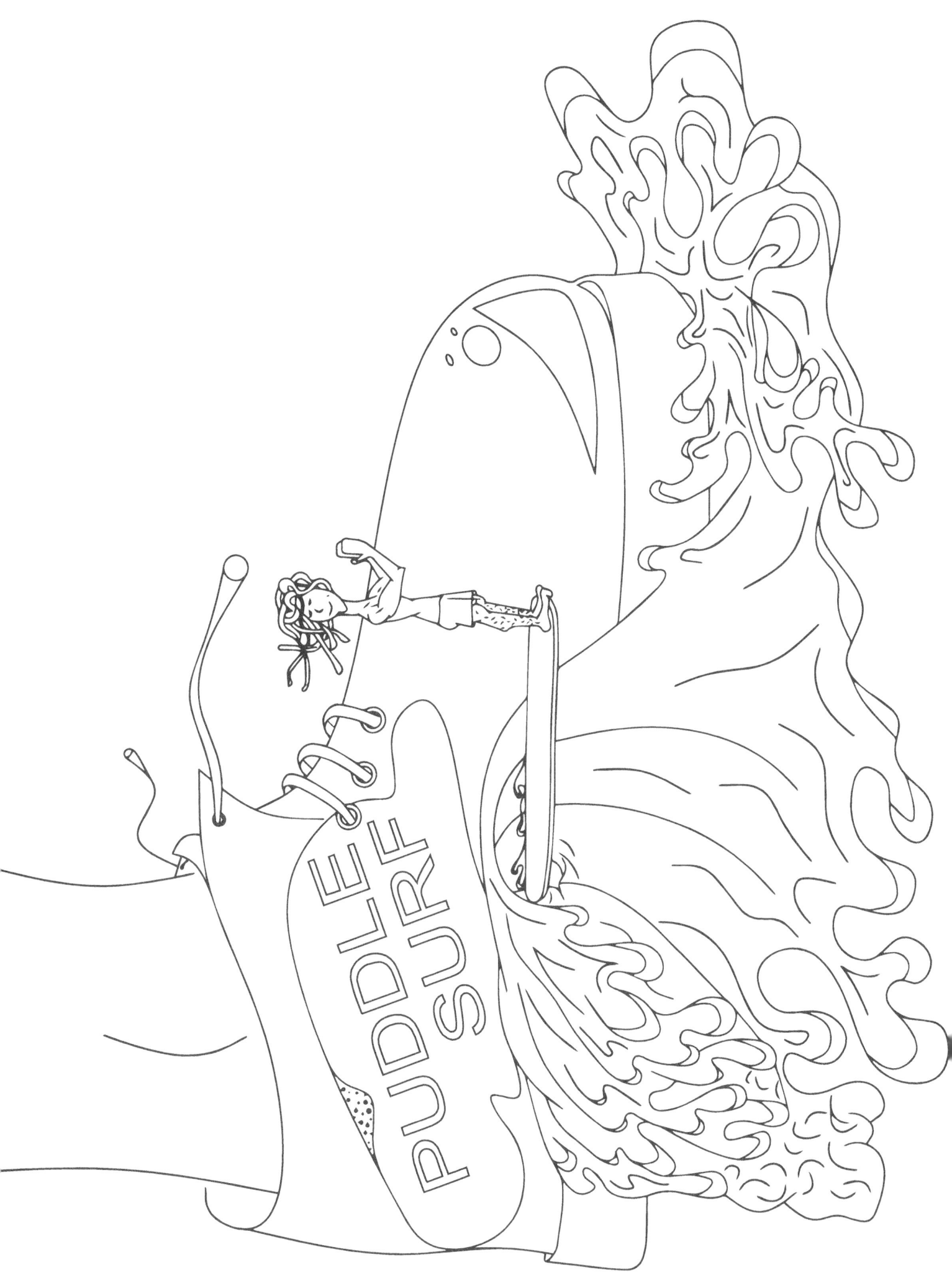

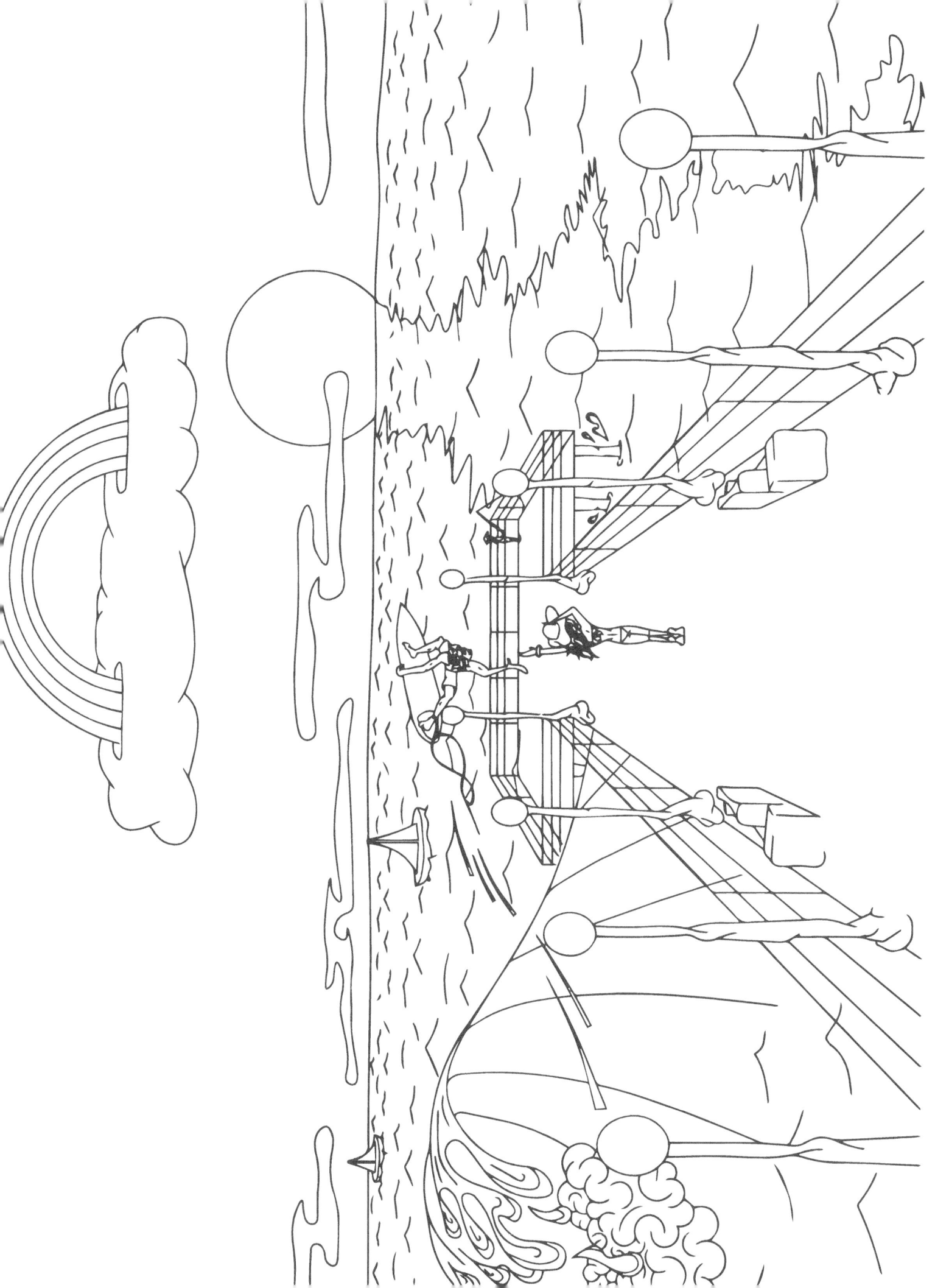

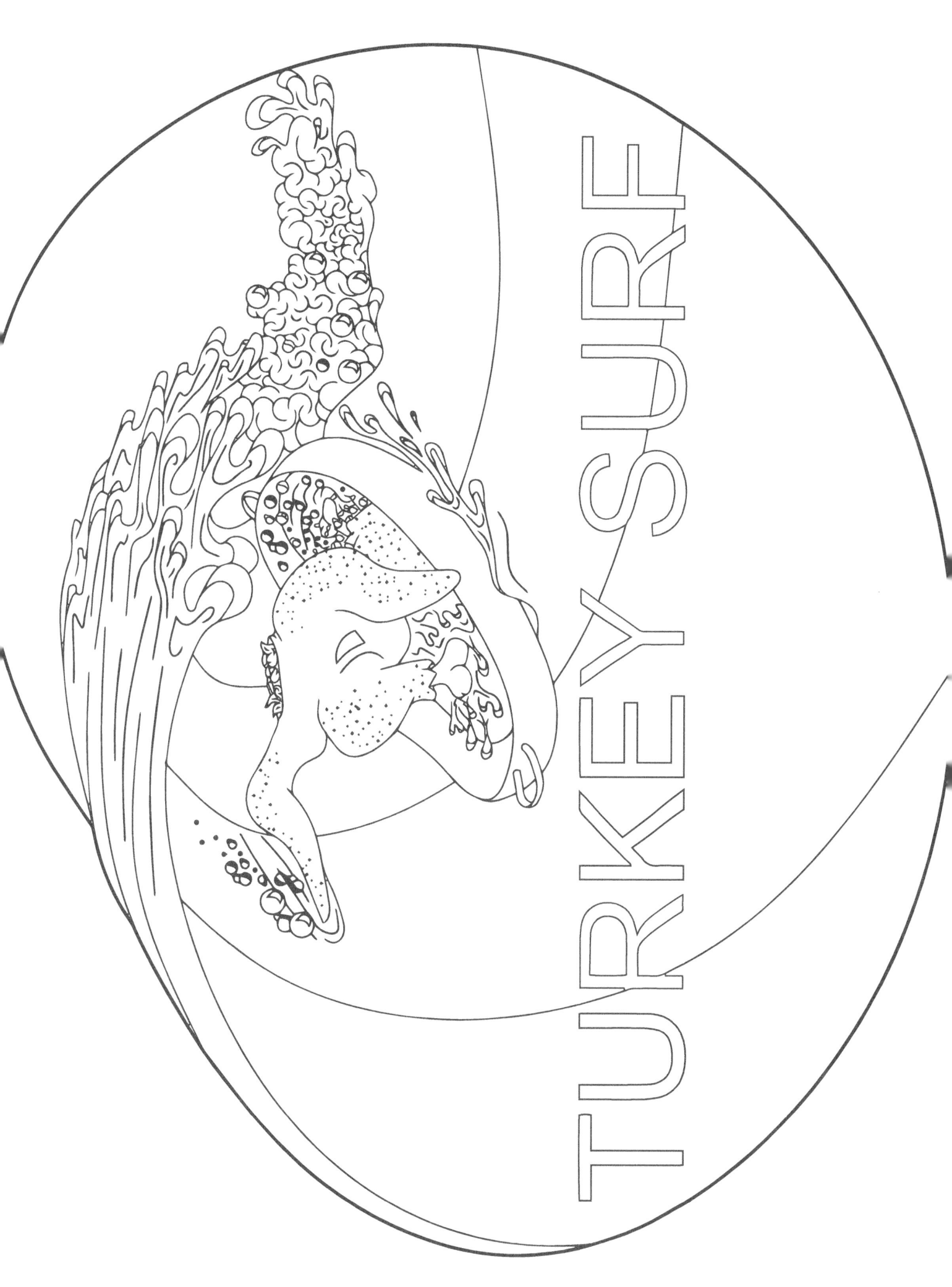

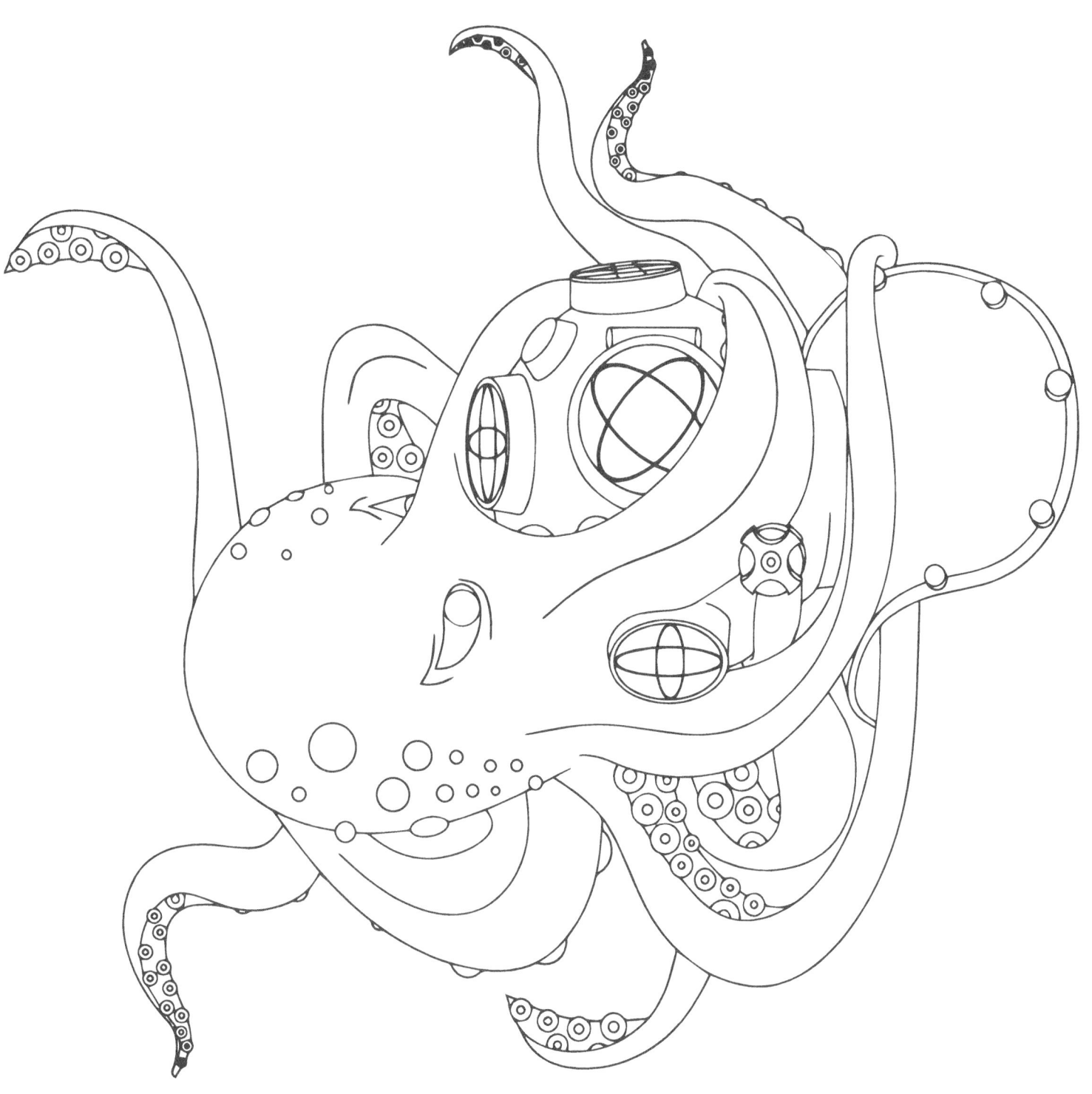

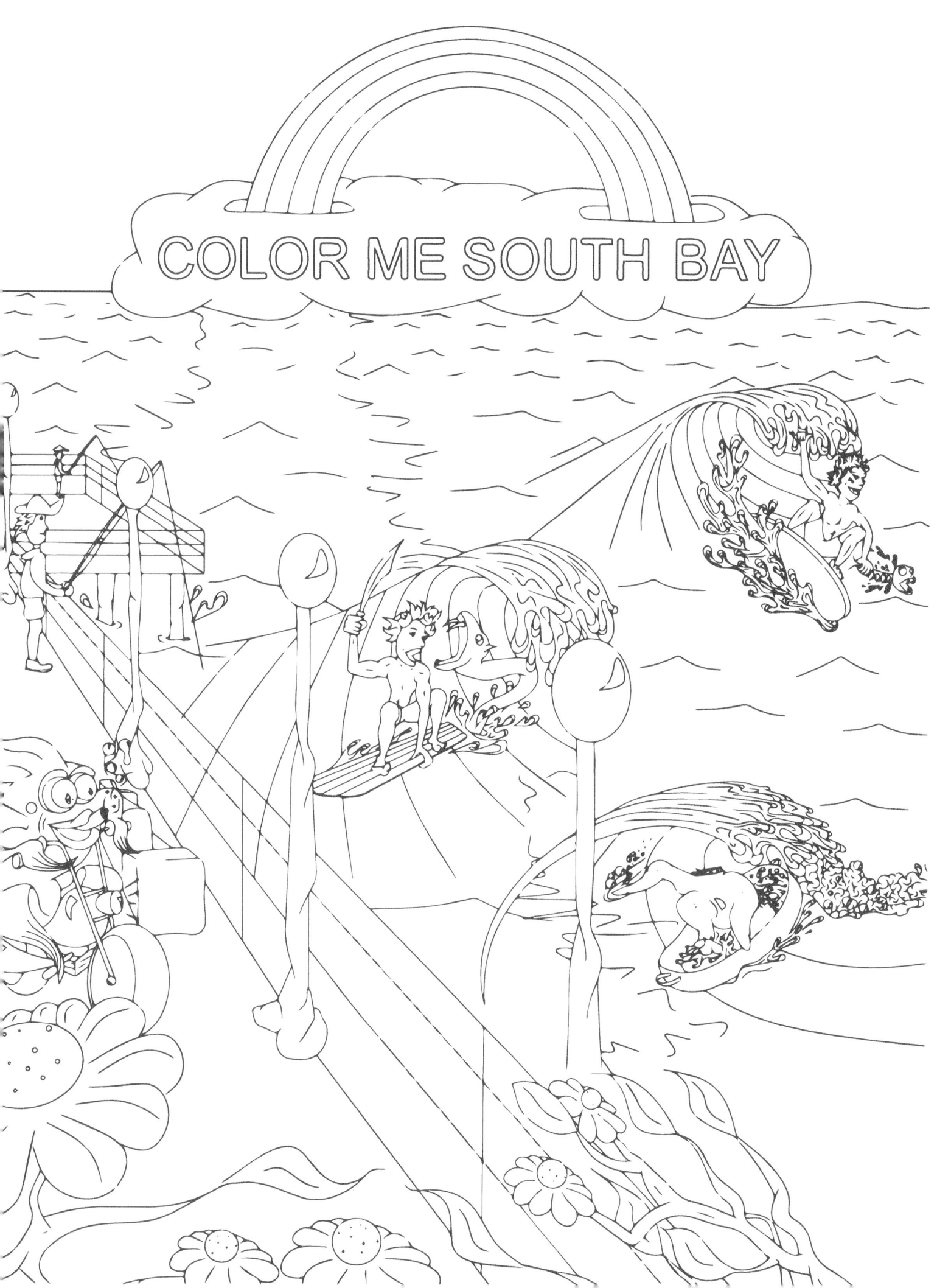

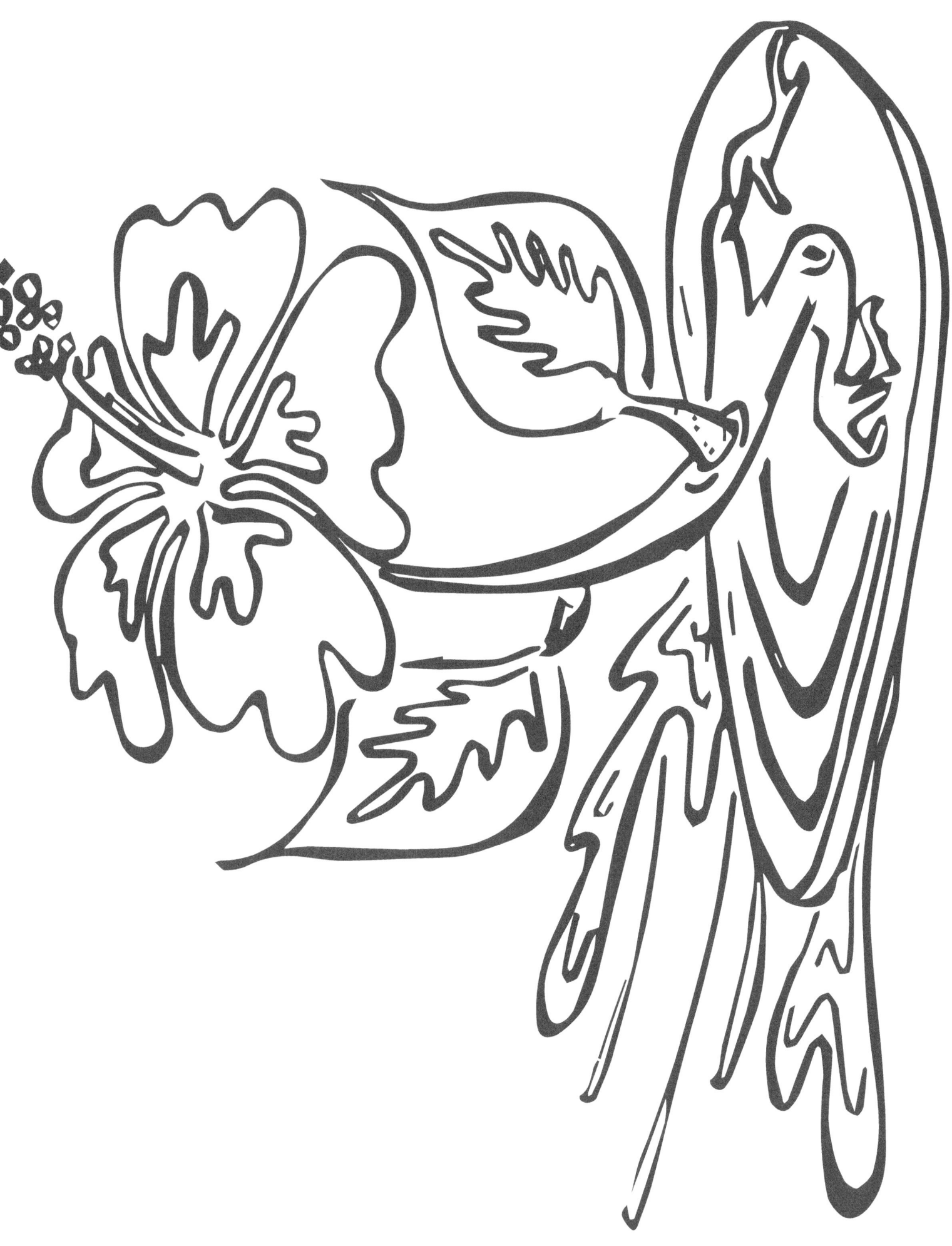

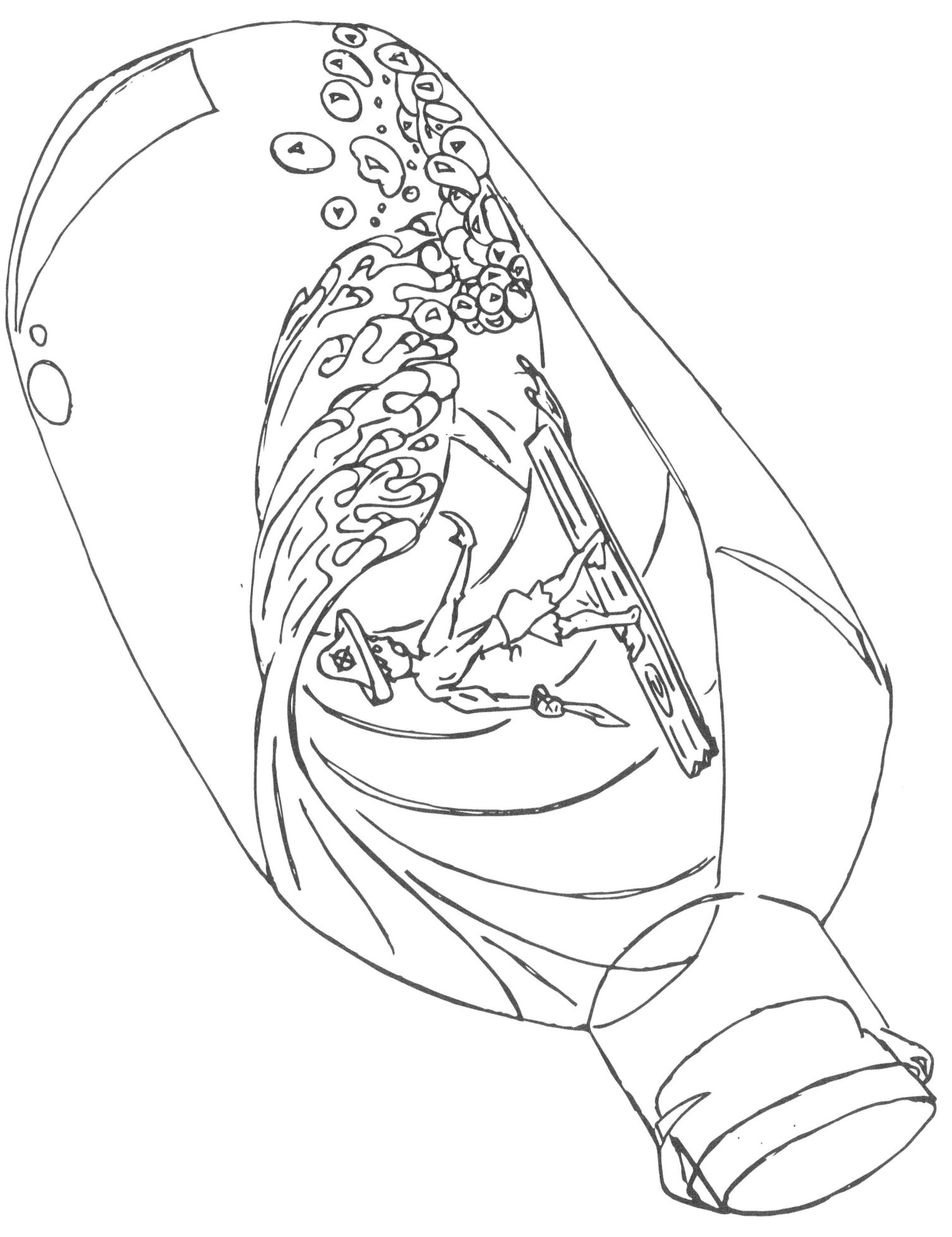

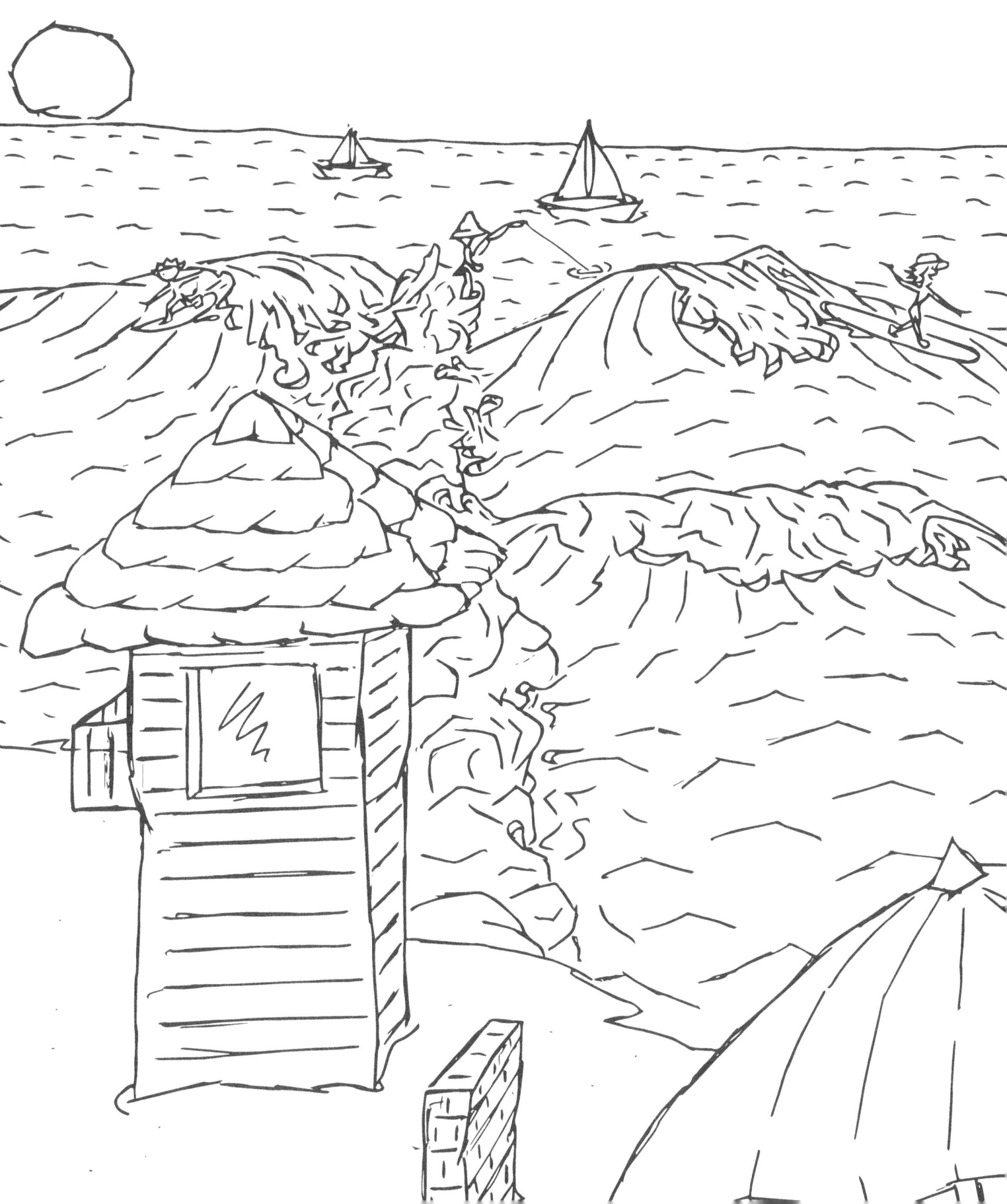